James Hector

Notes on New Zealand ichthyology

James Hector

Notes on New Zealand ichthyology

ISBN/EAN: 9783337866518

Printed in Europe, USA, Canada, Australia, Japan

Cover: Foto ©ninafisch / pixelio.de

More available books at **www.hansebooks.com**

ART. XXXIV.—*Notes on New Zealand Ichthyology.* By JAMES HECTOR, M.D., F.R.S., Director of the Geological Survey of New Zealand.

Plates X. and XI.

[*Read before the Wellington Philosophical Society, 25th July,* 1874, *and 10th Feb.,* 1875.]

LIST OF FISHES CAUGHT ON THE WEST COAST OF OTAGO, JANUARY–FEBRUARY, 1874.

	Preservation, Cuttle Cove.	Chalky, South Port.	Dusky, Pickersgill.
Oligorus gigas	...	...	*
Scorpis hectori	...	...	*
Chilodactylus macropterus	*	*	*
Latris hecateia	*	*	*
Mendosoma lineata	...	...	*
Latris ciliaris	*	*	*
Sebastes percoides	*	..	...
Scorpæna cruenta	*	*	*
Trachurus trachurus	...	...	*
Percis colias	*	*	*
Notothenia coriiceps (?)	...	...	*
Trypterygium varium	*	...	...
Labrichthys fucicola	*	*	*
„ bothryocosmus	*	...	...
„ psittacula	*	*	*
Odax vittatus	*	*	*
Coridodax pullus	*	*	*
Haplodactylus meandratus	...	...	*
Lotella bacchus	...	*	...
Pseudorhombus scaphus	*	...	...
Monacanthus convexirostris	...	*	*
Acanthias vulgaris	...	*	*
Mustelus antarcticus	...	*	*
Galeus canis	*	...	*
Bdellostoma cirrhatum	...	*	...

During the past year I have enjoyed several favourable opportunities of obtaining a further acquaintance with the fishes on the coasts of the colony, and particularly during a cruise in January last in his Excellency Sir James Fergusson's yacht Blanche round the south-west coast of Otago, in the course of which the trammel-net was frequently used in Preservation Inlet, Chalky Inlet, and Dusky Bay. Continuous observations of the temperature of the sea were also made, and it was found that at that season the surface of the sea on the East Coast and in Foveaux Strait averaged 56·5°, but on rounding the West Cape and in the Sounds the temperature of the surface water is 61°. From a few observations made with the Miller-Casella thermometer it was found that at from 17 to 25 fathoms depth on the West Coast, where the high surface temperature prevailed, the sea had the same temperature as the surface water on the East Coast. This appears to indicate that the warm Australian current is spread over the surface of this part of the ocean in a very thin stratum.

The above is a list of the fishes caught in the Sounds I have referred to. Frequently as many as 70 to 80 fish, of from 2 to 15 pounds weight, were obtained at a single haul of the net after it had been set for only an hour, the most abundant being the pakirikiri or rock cod (*Percis colias*), the tarakihi (*Chilodactylus macropterus*), and the wrasse (*Labrichthys fucicola*).

1* PLECTROPOMA HUNTII. sp. nov.
Pl. X.

B. 6; D. 10-20; P. 15; V. 1-5; A. 2-1-8; L.L. 50; L.T. 8|20.

Length equal to three times the height, head two and a half times in length; snout produced, lower jaw longest; base of spinous dorsal slightly exceeds that of the soft in length; upper jaw free, nostrils close to the orbits, anterior pair tubular.

Dorsal fin commences at one-third the total length, and over the posterior angle of the operculum; fourth spine longest, being twice the height of the first and last; soft dorsal of equal height; base of dorsal scaly, a scaly lobe extending to half the height of each spine in front.

Cleft of mouth oblique, equal to the height of longest dorsal spine, and twice the diameter of the eye, which is twice the interorbital width; upper maxillary broad and thin behind; teeth in villiform bands in both jaws, with six strong canines, two above and two below in the front, and one on each side in the lower jaw.

Præoperculum simple, ascending limb with minute denticulations, horizontal limb with two flat spines directed forwards; opercle with a superior notch, and a blunt membranous angle, with three flat sharp spines on the surface, the two lower being more distinct than the upper.

Pectoral rounded, with the middle ray slightly produced, extends to the commencement of the anal; ventrals shorter than the pectorals, and inserted slightly in advance of them; base of anal half the length of the soft dorsal; second spine thick and longer than the first ray, which is simple, being a slender spine adherent to the soft rays; fourth soft ray is the longest. Caudal equal in length to the ventral and rounded at the angles.

Scales moderate size, ctenoid. Lateral line curved.

Colour, red beneath, sides and back yellow, with dark patches of brown

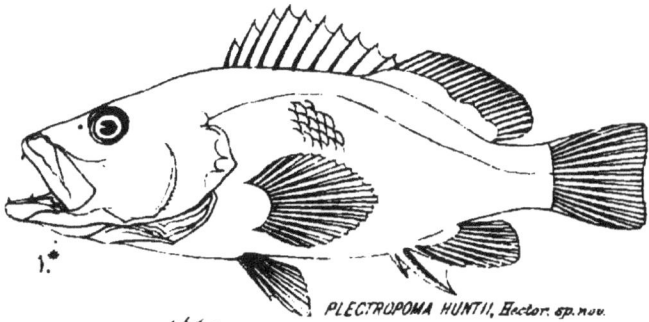

PLECTROPOMA HUNTII, Hector. sp. nov.

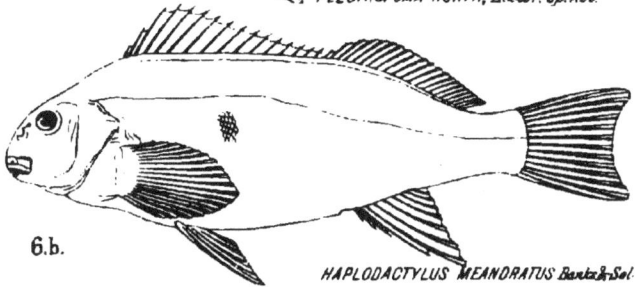

6.b.

HAPLODACTYLUS MEANDRATUS Bantz & Sol.

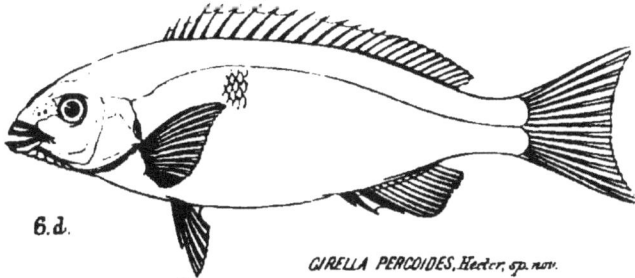

6.d.

GIRELLA PERCOIDES, Hector. sp. nov.

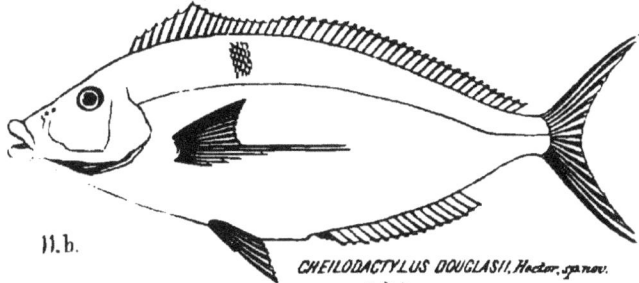

11.b.

CHEILODACTYLUS DOUGLASII, Hector. sp. nov.

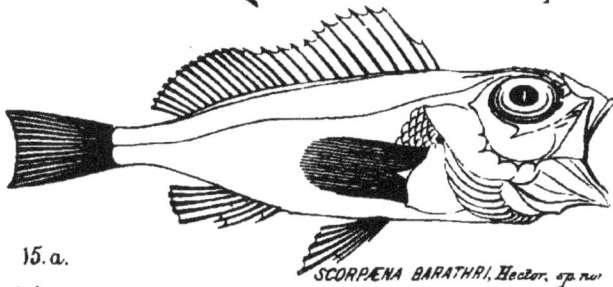

15.a.

SCORPÆNA BARATHRI, Hector. sp. nov.

J.B. del. et lith.

about the head, and several broad vertical bands of brown. A black spot on the snout.

Chatham Islands. Presented by F. Hunt, Esq.

This fish approaches *P. annulatus*, Günth. (I., 158), the habitat of which is unknown, but has one less branchiostegal, a more elongated form, spinous and soft dorsals of equal length, different number of fin rays, and greater development of second anal fin. In some of these respects it resembles *P. dentix*, Rich. (Voy. Ereb. and Terr., p. 117), which is from King George's Sound.

4a. SCORPIS FAIRCHILDI. sp. nov.
Native name—Mata.
S. hectori, Hutton, Trans. N. Z. I., V., p. 259, pl. vii.

Captain Hutton's description of the fish from the Bay of Plenty is very different from that of his original type from the West Coast Sounds, and a comparison of the specimens and further observation of the habits and appearance of the West Coast fish have convinced me that they are distinct species, and that the general outline of *S. hectori* is correctly given in pl. I., fig. 4, Cat. Fish. N. Z., while the figure quoted above is an equally correct representation of the second species, which I propose to name after Captain Fairchild, of the colonial gunboat Luna, who presented the specimen to the Colonial Museum.

In *S. hectori* the profile of the head descends abruptly, and the body is short, the height being contained only twice in the length; the pectoral fin is the same length as the head, and has the middle rays the longest. In many hundred specimens I have observed the round black spot on the side is always present. It is a beautiful fish when seen in the deep transparent water of the Sounds swimming about among the rocks in large shoals like gold-fish.

In *S. fairchildi* the shape of the body is fusiform and elongate, the height being only one third of the length; the abdominal cavity is one third of the length; the peritoneum having a nacreous lustre; œsophagus lined with brush-like tufts; stomach tubular, with a contracted pyloric branch reflexed at an acute angle; walls fleshy and rugose; seven pyloric appendages; liver small; intestines membranous, with many convolutions, being eleven times the length of the cavity. Generative organs (male) equal to stomach in length; air bladder large.

6b. HAPLODACTYLUS MEANDRATUS. Banks and Sol.
Pl. X.
Native name—Kehei.
Aplodactylus meandratus, Rich., Zool. Trans. III., 83.

$P.\frac{8}{5}-\frac{7}{7}$; D. 16·1/20; V. 1–5; A. II. 1/7; L.L. 176; L.T. 60.

Length equal to four and one third that of head, and to three times the height; body nearly round, thick in front; snout truncate, tumid, interorbital space convex; gape straight, almost inferior, its length being less than the interorbital distance; mouth has tumid reflexible lips; both jaws armed with several closely set rows of small tricuspid lancet teeth; patch of setaceous teeth on palate and on pharynx; tongue very short, smooth; four nostrils, anterior pair with tubular processes; præoperculum entire; operculum with a shallow notch; no pores about the head.

Both dorsals are set on a fleshy base; the two first spines of the dorsal are short, being less than the diameter of the eye; fifth spine is longest, and two and a half times in the height; fifth ray of soft dorsal the longest, and equal to spinous; length of soft dorsal is nine thirteenths of an inch.

Anal with fourth ray longest, the base being short by one third of first dorsal, with one spinous and one simple ray; caudal straight, the rays being equal to half the base of first dorsal; pectoral with six or seven simple and partly free rays, the middle ray being the longest; ventral with one thick simple ray and five divided rays, the third being the longest.

Scales small, oblong, cycloid.

Colour uniform, but darker above and about the head; rich olive-brown in vermiform marblings on a yellowish-grey ground, resembling a laminarian sea-weed encrusted with *Flustra* and *Spirorbis.*

Stomach elongated cylindrical, with thick rugose walls, and half the length of the abdominal cavity; liver forms a collar-shaped mass round the superior end; three short pyloric cæca; intestine membranous, and five times the length of the abdominal cavity; urinary organ very large, exceeding the liver in bulk; stomach and intestines full of corallines and sea-weed.

Largest specimen—total length, 22 inches.

The foregoing description is from several specimens caught in a trammel net by His Excellency the Right Hon. Sir James Fergusson, Bart.; Pickersgill Harbour, Dusky Bay, 3rd February, 1874.

This species resembles the fish described by Dr. Haast as *H. donaldii* (Trans. N. Z. I., V., p. 272); but there is no doubt that it is the same fish that was got by Captain Cook's expedition, figured by Banks and Solander and described by Sir John Richardson, as I have found it on all parts of the coast, and specially abounding round the headlands from the Kidnappers to East Cape where Captain Cook's specimen was obtained. It is caught in large numbers by the natives in the deep runlets excavated by the sea in the chalk marl strata which form the coast line, and for this purpose they use a peculiar net called the koko. This is a large scoop made with a bag-net suspended between two poles. With the rising tide this net is placed so as to block up one of the narrow runlets, and the fish are chased into the net from their hiding places among the kelp. Its flesh is coarse, with a rank flavour.

6c. HAPLODACTYLUS FERGUSSONI. sp. nov.

Native name—Hiwihiwi.

P. 6/8; D. 13/18; A. 3/6; V. 1/5; L.L. 60; L.T. 25.

Head three and a half times in the length and equal to the height; snout produced, profile concave, eyes prominent, their diameter being equal to half the gape; cheeks scaly; mouth deeply cleft, with thick lips; upper jaw formed by intermaxillaries; teeth minute, trenchant, lance-shaped, with single points in several rows on both jaws and a patch on the vomer; scales oblong, large, equal to half the orbit, cycloid, with six rays on attached margin.

Colour, grey-brown spotted with blue, white beneath.

Takes the hook, and is occasionally caught along with tarakihi. Stomach contained limpets and other shell-fish. Kawakawa Bay, East Cape, March, 1874.

Total length, 11 inches.

The six lower pectoral rays being simple, place this sparoid fish in the genus *Haplodactylus*, forming thus an exception to the other species of the genus, which are all vegetable feeders. The Maoris prize the hiwihiwi highly as food, considering it hardly inferior to the maomao (*Ditrema violacea*). I have dedicated this species to His Excellency Sir James Fergusson, to whom the Museum is indebted for many valuable specimens of the marine fauna of the New Zealand coasts.

6d. GIRELLA PERCOIDES. sp. nov.

Pl. X.

Black Perch.

B. 6; P. 15; V. 1/5; D. 15–12; A. 3–11; L.L. 58; L.T. 7/19.

Length three and one fifth times the height and four times that of head; orbital diameter equals half of snout and one-fifth of height of head; mouth protrusal with three imbricate rows of small teeth with blunt curved tips and a crowded belt of setaceous teeth on the inside of both jaws.

Dorsal begins behind the insertion of the pectoral and over the ventral; first soft dorsal ray is over the vent; base of the anal is less than the soft dorsal, its length exceeding by one half the height of the dorsal, which is one fourth the height of the body; second anal spine less than the third, the first being merely a slender process from the second, and not distinct in its insertion; caudal emarginate; lateral line arched; scales large, ciliate.

Colour (dried), olive-brown.

A single stuffed specimen in the Auckland Museum, labelled " Black Perch, Nelson."

Length, 16 inches..

It is a handsome fish in general form and size of scales, resembling the kahawai (*Arripis salar*). This fish differs but little except in its proportions from *G.* (*Crinideus*) *simplex*, Rich., and is evidently closely allied to that species which frequents the east coast of Australia.

11. *Chilodactylus spectabilis*, Hutton (Cat. Fish. N. Z., p. 8), is common near the East Cape, and is called by the natives Ehouhounamu or Nanua.

11b. **CHILODACTYLUS DOUGLASII.** Hector. nov. sp.

Pl. X.

Native name—Porae.

B. 6 ; P. 9/6 ; V. 1/6 ; D. 18–29; A. 3–16 ; L.L. 63 ; L.T. 7/18.

Head three and a half times in length ; height two and a half times ; body compressed, elevated, snout produced, profile above eyes abrupt, snout three and a half times the orbital diameter; fifth and sixth and lowest pectoral rays thickened and produced to opposite the ninth anal spine, fourth lowest extends to the vent ; anterior insertion of pectoral below the sixth dorsal spine, which is the highest of the series; soft dorsal commences over the vent, is uniform but not equal to the spinous in height, and extends further back on the tail than the anal ; ventrals below the tenth dorsal spine.

Thoracic region keeled, jugular with cross folds ; lips tumid ; teeth in a single series on intermaxillaries above, and on lower maxillaries small, trenchant and deeply imbedded in a fleshy gum ; cheek scaled ; horizontal branch of operculum smooth ; head and shoulder scales minute, body scales two thirds diameter of orbit, cycloid ; lateral line curved ; stomach with a deep fundus and pyloric branch equal in length to œsophagus, four short cæca ; intestine folded three times with a distinct spleen ; a distinct rectal division of the colon with strong muscular walls ; remainder of the intestine membranous ; abdominal cavity lined with black pigment; swim-bladder large and divided into lobes ; food, small *Crustacea*.

Colour, grey or green on back and head ; dorsal blue-grey with green spots ; cheeks silvery; gold and green patch on humerus and behind the gills ; back and sides of body green ; belly silvery ; fins steel blue.

Not a common fish, but highly esteemed as food. Caught along with tarakihi in ten to fifteen fathoms, but very local. Ngunguru Bay, north of Wangarei, and Bay of Islands, Auckland, in October. Only two caught among one hundred tarakihi.

Length, 2 feet.

I have named this fine species in honour of Sir Robert Douglas, Bart., to whose kind hospitality I was indebted for a pleasant fishing excursion at Ngunguru, which afforded me many novelties.

During the same visit to Ngunguru I obtained a mutilated fragment of the following fish, which appears to be well-known locally, but is rarely caught. I am unable to identify it with any described species.

Parore, or Mangrove Fish.

A fish 18 inches long with black bands on a dark ground ; head not seen ; anal short, 3–13 ; P. 15, all short ; height equal to half the length ; peritoneum black ; does not take bait, but frequents rocks among the mangroves at high water. Ngunguru and Wangarei Harbours.

15a. SCORPÆNA BARATHRI. sp. nov.
Pl. X.

B. 7 ; P. 18 ; V. 1/5 ; D. 11–1|13 ; A. 3/5 ; Pores 22 ; L. scales 65 ; L.T. 7/20.

Length equal to three and a quarter times the height, and two and two-thirds the length of head ; teeth on the palatines, vomer, and jaws in fine villiform bands ; general form compressed-elongate with profile of head convex ; length of snout equal to diameter of orbit, maxillary rather longer, inter-orbital space equals one-third the same ; supraorbital ridges with five spines ; Præoperculum with five spines on the lower limb ; suboperculum with two appressed spines on the upper limb ; third dorsal spine longest and equal to half the length of the head ; anal spine of same length and greater than base of anal fin ; the interval between the anal and caudal is twice that between the soft dorsal and caudal.

Colour silvery, with a yellow hue and a few brown spots on the back, and a dark patch on the dorsal fin.

Approaches nearest to *S. panda,* Rich., but is distinguished chiefly by the greater length and less height of the dorsal, and shorter pectorals.

Total length, 5 inches.

Dredged by H.M.S. Challenger Expedition in 400 fathoms, off Cape Farewell.

18a. TRACHICHTHYS INTERMEDIUS. sp. nov.
Pl. XI.

P. 16 ; V. 1/6 ; D. 6/13 ; A. 3/11 ; L.L. 28 ; L.T. 6–10.

Body compressed ; length of head nearly equal to the height and two and a half times in the length (without caudal, which is equal in length to the head); pectoral extends behind the vent, being same length as caudal, and has the fourth lowest ray longest ; ventrals slightly in advance of pectorals, and reach to the vent, which is behind the middle ; snout rounded, its length being one-half the diameter of the orbit ; cleft of mouth very oblique ; maxillaries expanded behind and twice the diameter of the orbit in length ; teeth in fine villiform bands ; interorbital space equal to the orbit, prismatic, with a lozenge-shaped space on each side, separated by a double elevated ridge that terminates in two spines over the nostrils in front and diverges behind to bound an occipital space ; the upper part of the head is formed of a delicate framework and membranes enclosing large cavities.

The infraorbital area is crossed by seven rays, and the operculum by two vertical ridges with five transverse bars, the lowest being prolonged over the suboperculum and angle of the gill-opening as a roughly serrated spine.

Between the occiput and commencement of the dorsal is a rough elevated ridge. The posterior dorsal rays rest in a groove. The caudal is deeply forked, each lobe consisting of ten soft rays and seven sharp spines above, and six below. The dorsal and anal fins end at the same vertical line, and the interspace to the caudal is equal to half the length of the body. The greatest height is in the vertical of the first dorsal. Dorsal begins at one-third the total length and over the origin of the ventral. The serrated ventral keel consists of ten scales.

Colour silvery white, except the tips of the dorsal fin and caudal lobes which are darkened with crowded black spots. The neck, back, and base of caudal have also a dark shade from the presence of minute spots. The scales above the lateral line are rough and adherent, but below are soft and deciduous.

Total length 2·7 inches. Height ·85.

Dredged by H.M.S. Challenger Expedition in 400 fathoms off Cape Farewell.

This fish approaches *T. elongatus*, Günth., of which a single specimen was obtained at the Great Barrier Island, but on account of its having evidently intermediate characters between that species and *T. australis*, I have distinguished it under the above name.

21A. ZIPHIUS GLADIUS. L.

Sword-fish.

Z. gladius, Günth., II., 511.

D. 3–40; A. 17; Ventral fins, none.

"The sword-shaped upper jaw much depressed and flat. Dorsal fin elevated in immature specimens. In old specimens the middle part of the dorsal and anal fins becomes very low or disappears so that there are two fins on the back and behind the vent."

My attention was drawn to a snout of this species in the Auckland Museum, which was obtained near Wangarei, to the north of Auckland. Being in that district I found on inquiry that the sword-fish was captured by the natives in Ngunguru Harbour, where it was seen swimming about in shallow water, with its dorsal fin high above the surface. The snout only was preserved, and given by the natives to Mr. McLeod, of Wangarei, by whom it was presented to the Auckland Museum. I record this statement as this sword-fish is mentioned only as an inhabitant of the North Atlantic, but is frequently brought out to the colonies and presented to museums.

24a. CARANX KOHERU. sp. nov.

Plate XI.

Native name—Koheru. The Herring Scad.

D. $7\frac{1}{20}$ I. A. $2\frac{1}{23}$ I.

Length of body is four and two third times the height and three and a half times the length of the head ; teeth very minute in a single series on both jaws, also present on the vomer and palatine bones ; cheeks smooth and bright silvery ; breast scaly ; lower jaw longest, maxillaries free, dependent and expanded ; snout longer than the diameter of the eye ; pectoral is over the ventral fin, and extends back to the vent, which is at one-half the total length, including the caudal ; scales very small, being one-fifth the diameter of the eye ; the lateral line is curved till under the twelfth soft ray of the dorsal, and then becomes straight, and is armed with fifty-eight keeled plates, the anterior curved portion having seventy-two serrated scales.

Colour, steel blue above, silvery beneath, with a black spot on the edge of the opercular notch.

Total length, 5·5 inches. The natives told me that the full adult size of this fish is 9 inches, and that it is found at all seasons along the coast between Wangarei and Cape Brett. I obtained my specimens among a shoal of immature hauturi (*Trachurus trachurus*) in Tutukaka Harbour, near Ngunguru.

31b. *Ditrema violacea*, Hutton.

Is a common fish near the East Cape and at the Bay of Islands for a few weeks in autumn, and is very much esteemed as food by the natives, who call it maomao.

31c. PLATYSTETHUS ABBREVIATUS. sp. nov.

Pl. XI.

B. 5 ; P. 16 ; V. 1/6 ; D. 7/26 ; A. 2/26 ; L.L. 80 ; L.T. 6/20 ;
Caudal, 3/ 14/3.

Body compressed ; general form rhomboidal, the greatest height being vertical to the second dorsal spine, which is over the anal spine ; length equal to one and two-third times the height, the head being two-thirds of the height ; length of snout less than diameter of the orbit, which is half the length of the head ; interorbital space equal to the snout, this being the greatest thickness of the body ; the eyes are very high up, and over each orbit is a double serrated ridge that ends in a spine that projects forwards and covers the nostril ; the inner branch of the ridge is continued backwards bounding a deep interorbital depression, the outer being continued round the margin of the orbit ; the lower jaw slightly projects ; the upper jaw is formed of the intermaxillaries, the maxillaries depending vertically over the angle of the mouth and ending in a spinous process ; the inferior edge of the lower jaw is serrate ; infraorbital space scaled, the opercula naked with all the lower free edges serrate.

A strong ridge with eighteen rough scales extends from the isthmus to the ventrals. The groove for the reception of the dorsal is bounded by twenty-six oblique spinous scales, and that for the anal by twenty similar scales each having four minute spines, the first being longest.

The first dorsal spine is short, the second long, being half the length of the head. The ventral spine is the same length, the anal spine being one-third. The second dorsal spine is compressed, with a sharp anterior edge. Soft dorsal does not begin with a spine.

The length of the caudal part of the body equals the orbital diameter, and has three short pointed spines above and below the base of the caudal, which is rounded. Scales very narrow and rough. Teeth very minute.

Colour silvery, with a black crescent behind the pectoral, which is very small and rounded. There is also a black line along the base of the dorsal and anal, and a patch on the base of the caudal.

The depressed interorbital space, shorter form, and different number of fin spines are the chief characters on which this fish is separated from the only other species of the genus—*P. cultivatus*, of which only two specimens are recorded from Norfolk Island.

Total length, 3 inches.

Dredged by H.M.S. Challenger Expedition in 400 fathoms off Cape Farewell.

32. *Scomber australasicus*, C. and V., is caught in large numbers on dark nights in spring between Wangarei and the Bay of Islands, where it is known as the Tawatawa.

36d. LEPTOSCOPUS ROBSONI. sp. nov.

P. 21 ; D. 34 ; A. 39.

Length equal to seven times the height, and four times the length of the head, which is two and a half times its greatest breadth ; the eyes are lateral and equal in diameter to the interorbital distance ; teeth in several rows, with a cluster of long incurved teeth in the middle of the upper jaw, and an irregular outer row of strong incurved teeth in the lower jaw ; vomer smooth, labial cirri hardly discernible. Colour grey, spotted with light-brown, light-grey beneath.

Length, 4·5 inches.

Cape Campbell. Collected by Mr. Robson, light-house keeper, in 1874.

This fish differs from *L. angusticeps*, Hutton, in the narrow interorbital space, the strong teeth, and almost total absence of cirri on the lip, but it might be the immature form of that species.

18.a.

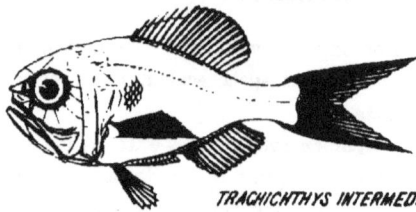

TRACHICHTHYS INTERMEDIUS, Hector. sp. nov.

24.a.

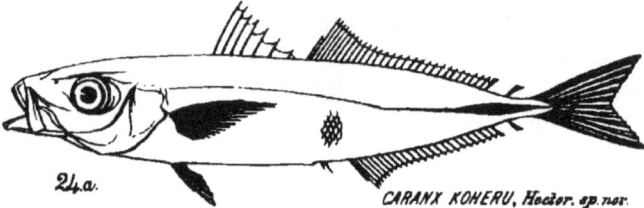

CARANX KOHERU, Hector. sp. nov.

31.c.

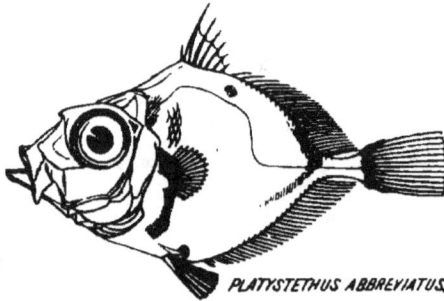

PLATYSTETHUS ABBREVIATUS, Hector. sp. nov.

78.a.

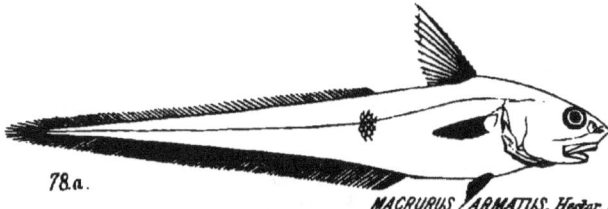

MACRURUS ARMATUS, Hector. sp. nov.

82.b.

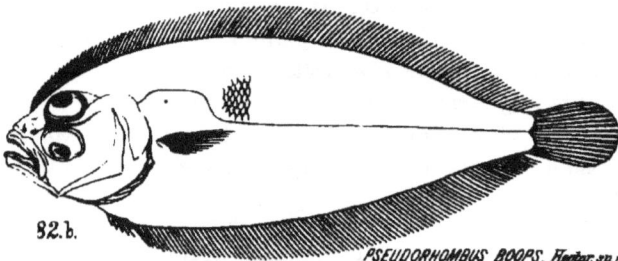

PSEUDORHOMBUS BOOPS, Hector. sp. nov.

90.d.

J.B. del. et lith.

MAUROLICUS AUSTRALIS, Hector. sp. nov.

.

www.ingramcontent.com/pod-product-compliance
Lightning Source LLC
Chambersburg PA
CBHW031159090426
42738CB00008B/1396